How Did Numbers Begin?

Numbers and counting have been basic to the development of civilizations, and this careful history for young readers introduces some of the fundamentals of our number system along with the story of how numbers probably began.

The Sitomers, experienced writers about mathematics for young children, have divided the story of numbers into five parts, including: matching; the concepts "as many as," "less than," "more than"; naming; ordering; and counting.

Using lively illustrations from prehistory to the present day, the authors have created an interesting and informative addition to the Young Math Series.

The beautiful pictures are by Richard Cuffari.

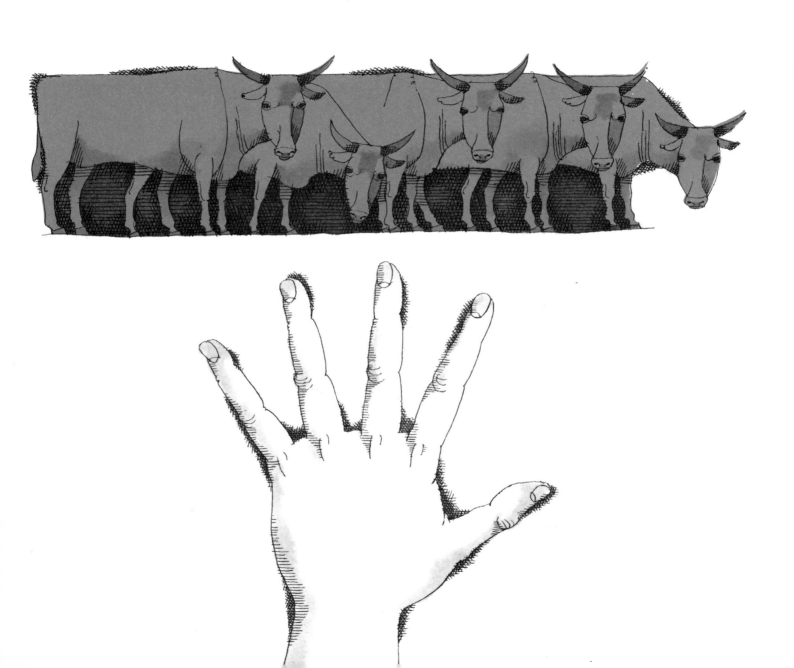

How Did Numbers Begin?

Mindel and Harry Sitomer

illustrated by Richard Cuffari

Thomas Y. Crowell Company
New York

YOUNG MATH BOOKS

Edited by Dr. Max Beberman, Director of the Committee on
School Mathematics Projects, University of Illinois

BIGGER AND SMALLER
by Robert Froman

CIRCLES
by Mindel and Harry Sitomer

COMPUTERS
by Jane Jonas Srivastava

THE ELLIPSE
by Mannis Charosh

ESTIMATION
by Charles F. Linn

FRACTIONS ARE PARTS OF THINGS
by J. Richard Dennis

GRAPH GAMES
by Frédérique and Papy

LINES, SEGMENTS, POLYGONS
by Mindel and Harry Sitomer

LONG, SHORT, HIGH, LOW, THIN, WIDE
by James T. Fey

MATHEMATICAL GAMES FOR ONE OR TWO
by Mannis Charosh

ODDS AND EVENS
by Thomas C. O'Brien

PROBABILITY
by Charles F. Linn

RIGHT ANGLES: PAPER-FOLDING GEOMETRY
by Jo Phillips

RUBBER BANDS, BASEBALLS AND DOUGHNUTS:
A BOOK ABOUT TOPOLOGY
by Robert Froman

STRAIGHT LINES, PARALLEL LINES,
PERPENDICULAR LINES
by Mannis Charosh

WEIGHING & BALANCING
by Jane Jonas Srivastava

WHAT IS SYMMETRY?
by Mindel and Harry Sitomer

Edited by Dorothy Bloomfield, Mathematics Specialist,
Bank Street College of Education

LESS THAN NOTHING IS REALLY SOMETHING *by Robert Froman*

STATISTICS *by Jane Jonas Srivastava*

VENN DIAGRAMS *by Robert Froman*

Library of Congress Cataloging in Publication Data. Sitomer, Mindel. How did numbers begin? (A Young math book.) SUMMARY: Briefly explains the matching and comparison of quantities, the naming and ordering of numbers, and counting—all steps in the history of numbers. 1. Numeration—History—Juv. lit. [1. Number systems] I. Sitomer, Harry, joint author. II. Cuffari, Richard, 1925– III. Title.

QA141.2.S53   513′.2   75-11756   ISBN 0-690-00794-9 (CQR)

3 4 5 6 7 8 9 10

How Did Numbers Begin?

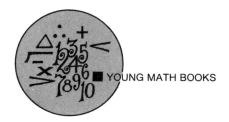

YOUNG MATH BOOKS

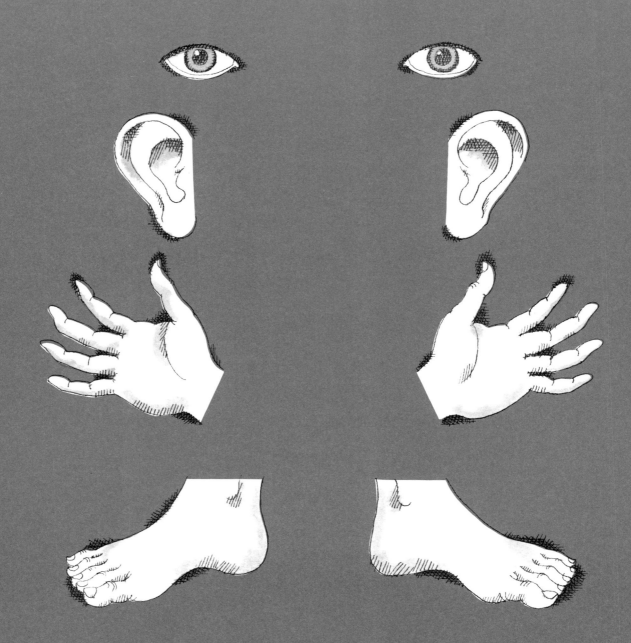

ONE, TWO	Buckle my shoe
THREE, FOUR	Shut the door
FIVE, SIX	Pick up sticks
SEVEN, EIGHT	Lay them straight
NINE, TEN	A big fat hen

Do you remember when you first learned to count to ten? Most children learn to count when they are very young. They learn how many eyes they have, and ears, and hands, and feet. Then they go on counting from there. There is a good reason for this.

INCHES 1 2 3 4 5 6 7

CENTIMETERS
1 2 3 4 5 6 7 8 9 10 11 12 13 14 15 16 17 18

Numbers are everywhere in our lives. We tell our age in numbers. We tell our height and weight in numbers. Our calendars tell us the date in numbers. All measurements use numbers. Even many of the games you play need numbers. Can you think of anything you used today that is not somehow connected with numbers?

When did people start using numbers? No one really knows, but numbers probably did not come all at once. The ideas about them must have developed slowly, perhaps in stages, and it all happened a very long time ago.

If you were living at that time you wouldn't have needed numbers very much. Your life might have been like that of some small groups of people who are still living in faraway lonely places. For food, they gather wild berries, roots, and fruit, and they may hunt or fish. Some of these people have names only for "one" and "two." Some say "two and one more" when they mean "three." Anything more than that is "many."

Imagine that you are living before numbers were invented. One day, while picking berries, you see a group of animals. It is important for the hunters to know about them, and you run to tell them. How can you tell them you saw seven animals? Remember, you know nothing about numbers or counting.

Or imagine that you are living at a time when your people have just learned to tame wild animals. They drive their herds out to pasture each day. Since they need these animals for food and clothing, it is important not to lose any.

You are the herder. You know nothing about numbers, and you cannot count. What can you do to make sure all your animals are back each night?

You might use a scheme like this: You put down a pebble for each animal as you drive it out to pasture. Later, you pick up a pebble for each animal that returns.

There is a tribe in Africa that believes it is bad luck to count its animals. It checks them by putting pebbles into a pouch.

Neither you nor the African tribe are counting animals. You don't know how many there are. You are matching them, one-to-one—one pebble to one animal. Each evening if there is an animal for each pebble, you know the whole herd is home.

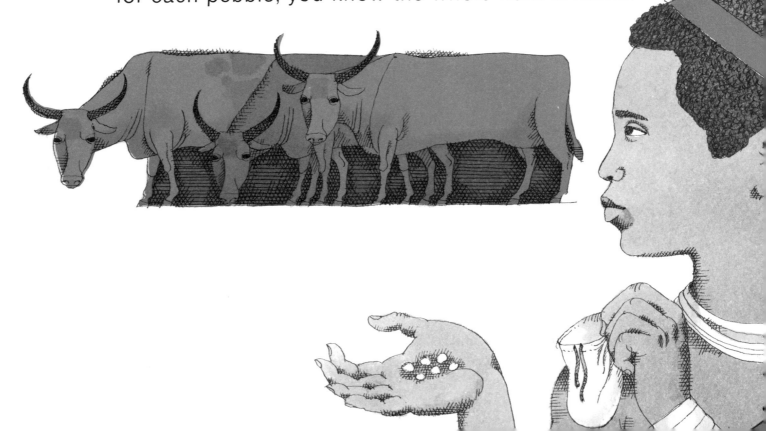

If you have one or more pebbles left over when your animals are back, you know you have to go out to look for the strays.

If you have one or more animals and no pebbles left to match them, you know you have a bigger herd than you started with.

Matching could have been the first important step in the story of numbers.

The second important step in the story of numbers might have come about from matching. It is these three ideas: "as many as," "less than," and "more than."

As many as: The set of animals and the set of pebbles matched, one-to-one.

Less than: There were not enough animals to match the pebbles.

More than: There were too many animals to match the pebbles.

These ideas are still used today, even though we know about numbers and counting.

Any game or dance where partners are chosen is a kind of matching. Do you know any games where matching is more important than counting?

Have you ever played Musical Chairs? In this game, children are matched with chairs. It isn't necessary to count the number of children or the number of chairs. There should be a chair for each child, but before the game starts, one chair is taken away.

The chairs are placed in two rows, back to

back. Music is played and the children march around the chairs. When the music is suddenly stopped, the children sit down. But one child will have no seat. That child is out of the game, and another chair is taken out, too. The game goes on until there are two children and only one chair. The child who gets the last seat wins the game.

The third step in the story of numbers also probably came from matching. It is the naming of numbers.

If the people of long ago did match sets of objects, like pebbles and animals, they must have noticed that two pebbles always matched two eyes, or two ears, or two hands, or two feet, or even the two wings on a bird. Perhaps one day when someone was talking about two animals he had no pebbles handy. He might have pointed to his eyes to mean "As many animals as I have eyes." After a while, his people may have realized that they could do without pebbles. They could point to their eyes whenever they wanted to talk of a pair of anything. Probably later, they even stopped pointing. The word for "eyes" was enough to mean "two."

We are fairly sure this is how it must have happened in parts of China because there the word for two is the same as the word for eyes. In Tibet, the word for two is the same as the word for ears.

So we see that the third step, naming numbers, probably came from using the same word for a set of objects (like eyes) and for a number (two).

How was "one" named? We think most people used it instead of the word "a." If you had only one animal, you would not need to put down a pebble to know that your animal came back.

You could always remember one. And so, a cow, a bird, or a tree, became one cow, one bird, or one tree.

We do not know how any people named "three." The name might have come from a matching set of objects, or it might have come from "two and one more."

In trying to trace how numbers were named, "five" is the only other number we are sure of. Most people of long ago named five for the fingers they have on one hand. There are some languages where the word for five and the word for hand is the same. A long time ago in our own West, in Indian picture writing, a hand drawn next to a picture of a tree meant five trees.

Do you remember the question on page 5? When you ran to tell the hunters about seven animals you had seen, you might have matched each animal with a pebble or a stick, and carried them to the hunters. Or you might have used your hands to mean you had seen animals to match "one hand (five fingers) and two more fingers."

It seems natural to use our fingers in matching and counting, and we believe almost all people once did. Children still like to count this way, and many grownups do, too.

Naming numbers larger than five depends on whether or not you count by fives. If you count by five, then the name for six is five and one. The name for seven is five and two, and so on to ten, which is named two fives. Eleven then becomes two fives and one. Some people in Africa count this way. Mathematicians call this using the base five.

But we have two hands, or ten fingers. That is probably the reason most people count by tens, using the base ten. This is why in our money system there are ten pennies in a dime, and ten dimes in a dollar.

In using the base ten, each number from one to ten must have its own name. We have already named the first five numbers, but we also need the names six, seven, eight, nine, and ten.

We don't know how these numbers were named and they have different names in different parts of the world. But here is something interesting for you to think about. The **ideas** of numbers such as two, three, or seven are the same, no matter what **name** each has. Three is always one more than two, and seven is always one more than six, whatever its name is in any language.

Once the first ten numbers in base ten were

named, it was not hard to name the rest of the numbers. You can see how thirteen and fourteen came from three and ten, and four and ten. Eleven and twelve take a little studying. Once the word for eleven meant ''one left over when counting by tens.'' Twelve can be traced to an old German word, ''zwo-lif,'' which means two and ten.

Can you tell how the rest of the teens got their names?

But how about twenty? "Two tens" became twenty and "three tens" became thirty, and so on.

What happens when you get to a hundred (100)? Instead of saying one hundred twenty-three, as we do, you could say ten tens and twenty-three. But that is a very long name for a number. People long ago thought so, too, and they gave the name "hundred" to ten tens.

A new name was given to ten hundreds, too. You know it as a thousand (1,000). Do you know another name for a thousand thousand (1,000,000)?

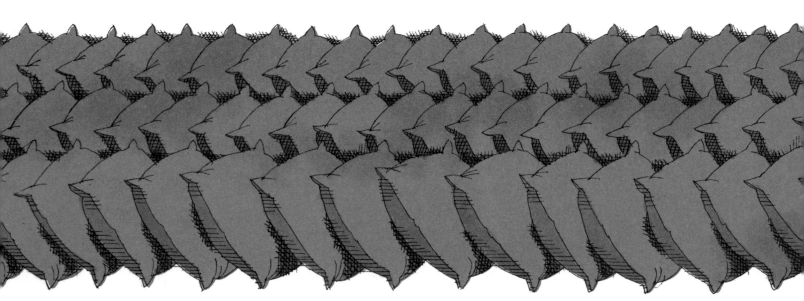

27

The naming of numbers is only a part of the story of how numbers began. It is not all that the people of long ago needed to know before they could count. If you wanted to count to ten would you count

8, 7, 4, 5, 9, 1, 3, 6, 2, 10?

Of course not. As you did in the nursery rhyme, you would say

1, 2, 3, 4, 5, 6, 7, 8, 9, 10.

Do you know why?

Numbers must be put into their proper order before they become counting numbers. *And this is the fourth step in our story of numbers.*

The order of counting numbers follows a very simple rule. Two is one more than one, three is one more than two, nine is one more than eight, twenty-two is one more than twenty-one. . . . Can you figure out the rule?

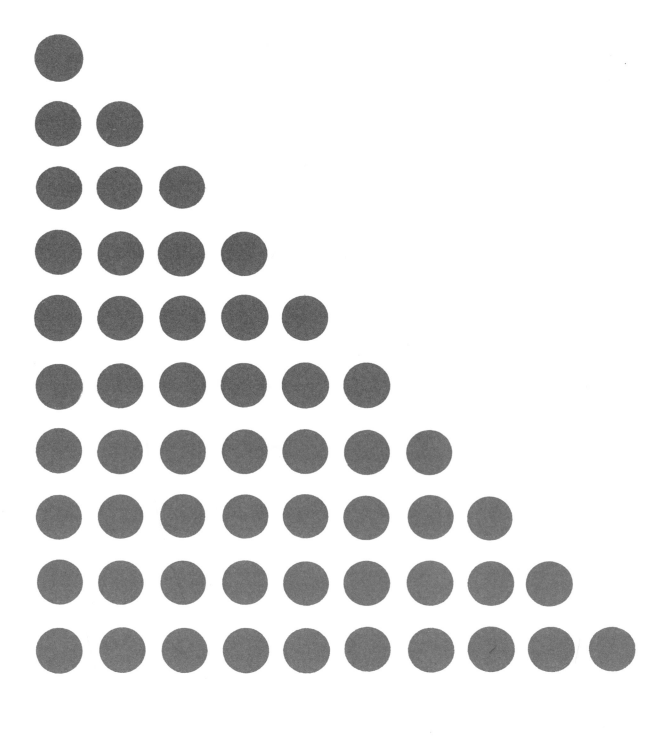

The next number in counting numbers is always one more than the number just before it.

Last of all, is the fifth step in our story of numbers: counting.

Counting is nothing more than a special kind of matching. It is matching a set of objects with a set of numbers, but the set of numbers must start with one, and be in their proper order. To count the balls in this set, each ball is matched with its properly ordered number, like this:

5 6 7 8

The last number reached in the matching
tells how many.

When you are having a party, do you have to take all the children to the store to match each child with an ice-cream cone? All you need to know is how many. When you know how many children are coming, you will know the number of ice-cream cones to buy.

When people learned how to count, they found a very important tool that was to change their lives. It helped them in trading. It helped them to measure and make things, and to keep records. It is one of the tools that helps make living, as we know it today, possible.

ABOUT THE AUTHORS

How Did Numbers Begin? is the fifth book on which Mr. and Mrs. Sitomer have collaborated. Harry Sitomer, educated in New York City, has taught mathematics in high school and colleges and is an author of textbooks for several experimental mathematics syllabi related to the "new math." He is a coauthor of a textbook on linear algebra. He is also an enthusiastic cellist and gets much enjoyment from his regular sessions with amateur string quartets.

Mindel Sitomer, also educated in New York City, as a biologist, found that their own two children and seven grandchildren had no difficulty in understanding large scientific concepts at an early age. Hence her enjoyment in working with her husband on these books for young readers. She also brailles books for blind children.

The Sitomers make their home in Huntington, New York.

ABOUT THE ILLUSTRATOR

Richard Cuffari's paintings have been exhibited in several New York galleries. A number of his illustrations have appeared in the design shows of the American Institute of Graphic Arts and in the annual exhibits of the Society of Illustrators.

A native of New York, Mr. Cuffari studied at Pratt Institute. He lives in Brooklyn with his four children.